GW00870224

Praying with the friends of Jesus

Juliette Levivier

Illustrations by Anne Gravier

CTS Children's Books

Table of Contents

Come and meet Jesus

Jesus met a lot of people along the roads of the Holy Land. Crowds of people came to hear him speak about God. In spite of the large number of people he met, he saw each person as an individual. Each person had all his attention and all his love. Each face, each name was unique for him.

We can get to know Jesus through all these witnesses. He is someone who forgives, who heals, who feeds, who calls all those he loves - which means everyone in the world.

Jesus invites you to meet him too.

He is looking at you, calling you, saving you. He loves you too.

Come and pray with the friends of Jesus

Settle down comfortably: in order to pray, you need to keep still. Whether you choose to sit or kneel, your body is praying too.

Begin by making the sign of the cross.

Choose one of the people in this book. Look carefully at the picture, then read the smaller text on the left-hand page, by yourself or with a grown-up. Then close your eyes. Imagine that you are one of Jesus's friends and then imagine the scene. What is happening ? What is Jesus saying ? What is he doing ?

Slowly read the extract from the gospel, and then the prayer written in red.

You can make your prayer last longer with the words and ideas you are carrying deep in your heart. Jesus is there, listening to you.

Simeon

Joseph and Mary came to the Temple in Jerusalem to present Jesus to God. An old man called Simeon welcomed them. Taking Jesus in his arms he began to praise God, saying:

> *My eyes have seen the salvation which you have*
> *prepared for all the nations to see,*
> *a light to enlighten the nations*
> *and the glory of your people, Israel.*
>
> Luke 2:30-32

Simeon had waited a long time for the Saviour promised by God. But how did he recognise him in this tiny baby ? Very easily, because he let himself be guided by the Holy Spirit.

How can we recognise Jesus today ? By paying attention to everything that is beautiful, simple, true and pure in each person.

Lord Jesus, you came for all the
peoples of the earth.
May all those who are waiting
for you, recognise you.
Put into my heart the desire to see you.
Put into my heart the joy of knowing you.
Put into my heart your light.

John the Baptist

What a strange man John the Baptist was !
He wore a camel skin. He was as thin as a rake.
He ate honey and locusts. He stayed away from towns
and villages but crowds of people still came to see
him. God had given him a very special mission. He
was to baptise in the River Jordan all those who were
waiting for the Messiah to come. He said to them:

> *Prepare a way for the Lord.*
> *Make his paths straight.*

Luke 3:4

He called them to change their hearts, to convert
and to leave their sins behind so that they could
welcome Jesus, the Messiah, when he came.

How can I prepare to receive Jesus ?

John the Baptist,
you baptised Jesus
and led so many disciples to him.
Light the way for all those
who are looking for Jesus.
Look after all those who have received
the life-giving waters of baptism.

The first disciples

Jesus was walking on the shores of Lake Galilee.
He saw fishermen throwing their nets out into the
water. He called to them:

"Follow me and I will make you fishers of men."
And they left their nets at once and followed him.

Matthew 4:19-20

At once Simon, Andrew, James and John stopped
what they were doing, left everything and joined Jesus.
Jesus touched their hearts and so they changed their
lives. These men became Jesus's closest friends.

Jesus calls me too. If I answer his call every day,
my life will be full of joy !

Here I am, Lord Jesus ! I'm coming !
I know you're calling me.
You can count on me.
I offer you my heart and my life.
Give me the joy and the strength to be
a faithful disciple.

11

Matthew

Matthew was a tax collector. He didn't have a good reputation because people believed tax collectors took money that didn't belong to them. Nevertheless, Jesus noticed him and called him:

"Follow me." And he got up and followed him.
Matthew 9:9

Jesus did not judge by appearances. He knew this man wanted to lead a different life. Matthew himself understood that for this to happen he would have to leave everything and follow Jesus.

I can get stuck in my bad habits, but Jesus knows that I can change and he gives me the strength to do so.

Matthew, you were very brave !
You left everything to follow Jesus.
You learned to share and to love.
Please help me not to tell lies,
and not to cheat or be lazy,
and to follow Jesus
and live by his Word.

Mary at Cana

Jesus and Mary were invited to a wedding. In the middle of the meal, Mary realised that there was no more wine ! The celebrations would be ruined. At once she told Jesus: "They don't have any wine left !" She knew he could save the day, so she said to the servants:

Do whatever he tells you.

John 2:5

Then Jesus changed the water which the servants had brought him into wine - and very good wine at that ! That was his first miracle. Thanks to Mary speaking to her son, the young couple and their friends could go on rejoicing.

We too can always count on Mary to intercede for us with Jesus. All we have to do is share our secrets, our desires and our prayers with her.

Mary, lead me to Jesus, your son.
You are a light for my steps,
a guide on the way.
When I am near you
I am not afraid of anything.
I want to do everything Jesus tells me,
and I need you to help me...

The leper

A leper met Jesus on the road and fell to his knees
in front of him. He begged Jesus to heal him because
he trusted in him.

*Feeling sorry for him, Jesus stretched out his hand
and touched him. "Of course I want to heal you !"
he said. And the leprosy left him at once
and he was cured.*

Mark 1:41-42

Leprosy is a terrible disease... It disfigures people who
have it. Everyone believed it was very easy to catch it so
they all ran away. But Jesus was not afraid. He touched
the leper, and his touch, so full of compassion, cured him.

There are some people I treat like lepers, and who
I think are not worth talking to. Is this how Jesus
thinks of them ? Of course not! So why don't I
change my way of looking at them, and try to see
them as Jesus does ?

Lord Jesus, you did not shrink
away from the leper.
You went to him and you touched him.
You do the same to everyone.
Each one of us is beautiful in your eyes,
each one has a place in your heart.
No one is outside your love.

17

The paralytic

There was a paralysed man whose friends wanted
to bring him to Jesus to be cured, but there were so
many people in front of the house where Jesus was
that they could not get through...
So they climbed up onto the roof, pulled off the tiles,
and lowered the stretcher down right in front of Jesus !

*Seeing their faith, Jesus said to the paralytic, "My
son, your sins are forgiven… Get up, pick up your
stretcher, and go off home."*

Mark 2:5-12

The paralytic's friends were so clever and brave !
Nothing could stop them ! Jesus was moved to see
how generously they helped their friend...

It is my sins that paralyse me and stop me walking
towards Jesus. With the help of my parents, my
catechists and the priests I know, I can come to
Jesus and be set free.

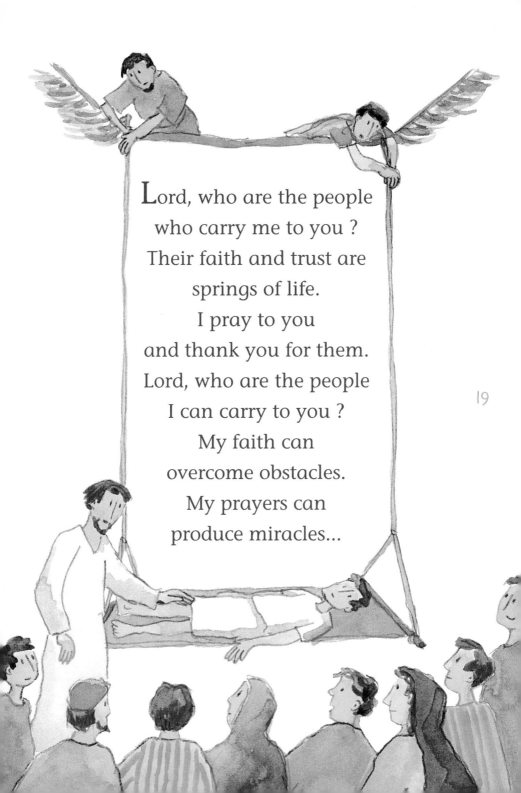

Lord, who are the people
who carry me to you ?
Their faith and trust are
springs of life.
I pray to you
and thank you for them.
Lord, who are the people
I can carry to you ?
My faith can
overcome obstacles.
My prayers can
produce miracles...

19

The Samaritan woman

Jesus was tired and sat down by a well. A woman come to draw water. Jesus asked her to give him a drink. He was thirsty for a drink of cold water. The Samaritan woman was thirsty for love. She quickly understood that Jesus was not an ordinary man...

Anyone who drinks the water that I shall give will never be thirsty again: the water that I shall give will turn into a spring inside him, welling up to eternal life.

John 4:13-14

She had come to get water from the well and instead she left with faith ! She was so happy she even forgot her jug as she went to find her friends so they could meet Jesus too.

Meeting other people can be difficult, especially people who are different from me. Sometimes, when I have helped someone, I realise that actually they have helped me !

The water which gives me life
is the water of my baptism.
The water which makes me grow
is the water of your Word.
Yes, Lord, I am coming to you,
I am coming to the well where
you are waiting for me.
My God, I am thirsty for your love,
I am thirsty for your truth.

The crowds

Jesus found a quiet place to rest with his disciples, but a huge crowd came and joined him. So he spoke to them for a long time about the Kingdom of God, and about justice and peace.

But it got late and the crowd must have been hungry. How could they feed so many people ? A small boy had five loaves and two fish. Jesus took them and blessed them and broke the bread.

They all ate as much as they wanted.

Mark 6:42

My body needs bread to grow. There's never any danger that I might forget to eat ! But what about my soul ? It needs to be fed too or it will shrivel up ! It is hungry for the Word of God and the Eucharist...

Lord Jesus, give us our daily bread.
It feeds our body and gives us the
strength to work.
Give us the bread of your Word.
It feeds our heart and gives us
the strength to go on.
Lastly, give us the bread
of your Eucharist.
It feeds our soul and gives
us the strength
to love.

Peter

Jesus asked his disciples:

> *Who do you say that I am ?*

Peter answered:

> *You are the Christ, the Son of the Living God.*

So Jesus said to him:

> *You are Peter and on this rock I will build my Church.*

Matthew 16:15-18

Peter was not perfect or even very wise but he was a man with an open heart. God himself had revealed to Peter who Jesus was. And, because he had a simple heart, Peter was able to believe the unbelievable ! Jesus entrusted his people, the Church, to Peter. The church, where we go to mass, is the "house" of the Christians in our area, our town. The Church Jesus spoke about is the people, the children of God throughout the centuries, on earth and in heaven.

Since my baptism, I have belonged to the people of God. The Church needs me to announce the Good News. How can I serve her from now on ?

Peter, your faith is as solid as a rock !
Jesus gave you the mission
of leading his flock.
I pray to you for our Pope, your successor,
and for the bishops and priests.
Help them to stay faithful
to what Jesus wants.
Help all Christians to remain
united in love and faith.

25

Martha and Mary

Martha and Mary, the two sisters of Lazarus, loved Jesus very much and were always very happy to have him in their house.

Mary sat at Jesus's feet. She was open and attentive to his words. She listened to him with her whole heart.

> *Mary... sat down at the Lord's feet*
> *and listened to him speaking.*
>
> Luke 10:39

Martha was in the kitchen preparing a good meal. But she was so busy that she ended up forgetting about Jesus. She didn't have time to listen to him, and her heart was closed. She was unhappy because her sister wasn't helping her... and she told Jesus off !

Wasn't she cheeky to tell Jesus off !
Am I sometimes tempted to do the same ?

Some days I get everything ready to pray,
a candle, some flowers, a picture
– but my heart is far away.
I'm restless and I think about
lots of other things.
Forgive me, Lord. You're here,
you're speaking to me and I ignore you.
Help me listen to your Word.
Help me to welcome your presence.

Zacchaeus

There was a huge crowd in Jericho ! Zacchaeus was a very rich but very short man. He wanted to see Jesus too but he didn't dare mix with the rest of the crowd because the people of the town didn't like him. So he decided to climb a tree. That way he could see Jesus without being seen himself ! But sure enough, Jesus stopped, looked up at him and said:

Zacchaeus, come down. Hurry, because I must stay at your house today !

Luke 19:5

Zacchaeus jumped for joy ! It's true he had been dishonest, but he was not afraid to admit it in front of Jesus and everyone else. He was sorry and he decided to undo the wrong he had done. His heart and his life were changed, and he was tremendously happy.

I would really like to see Jesus, just as Zacchaeus did. I have to prepare my heart to receive him...

Lord, I am not very big or strong.
I'm not so clever.
But even so, you still see me and love me.
You call me by my name.
You enter my life every day
and light it up with your love.

Bartimaeus

Blind Bartimaeus was sitting at the side of the road and, as Jesus walked by, he called out to him. He shouted out aloud, so loudly that the other people were trying to keep him quiet. But Jesus heard him and called back to him. Bartimaeus jumped up, full of joy: he was sure Jesus could give him back his sight.

Then Jesus spoke, "What do you want me to do for you ?" "Rabbuni", the blind man said to him, "Master, let me see again." Jesus said to him, "Go, your faith has saved you."

Mark 10:51-52

And in fact, Jesus did cure him ! He saw the light of day, and from then on his light was Jesus.

For me too, there are days when I don't see anything, when I'm sad and feel like I'm in the dark. There are other days when everything I see is beautiful and filled with light and this makes me truly happy.

Open my eyes, Lord,
so that I can see your Light.
Open my ears, Lord,
so that I can hear your Word.
Open my heart, Lord,
so that I can welcome your love.

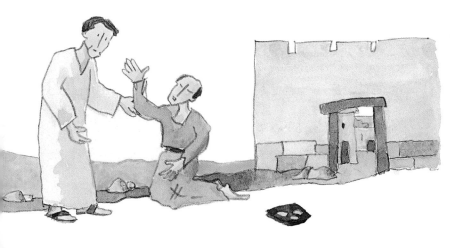

The rich young man

A young man asked Jesus what he had to do to have eternal life. He had a good heart. He was upright and just. He really wanted to follow Jesus because he realised that he is the way that leads to God.

Jesus looked steadily at him and loved him, and he said... "Go and sell everything you own and give the money to the poor, and you will have treasure in heaven; then come, follow me."

Mark 10:21

Jesus's answer overwhelmed him. He was very rich! What Jesus asked him seemed too hard and so he was very, very sad.

It is difficult to follow Jesus... Sometimes my possessions keep me far away from him. However, my real riches come from my heart and not from what I own. And even though I have a good heart, sometimes I don't always manage to do good things...

Lord, you look steadily at me
and you love me.
My only wealth is you.
My only treasure is your love.
My only happiness is to live
with you forever.
Make me open to your call.
At your side I will find joy.

Those who rejected Jesus

There were also a lot of people who rejected Jesus. Their hearts were firmly shut against him. They were closed in their own ideas and they didn't want to change anything in their lives or behaviour. Nothing brought them close to Jesus, not even the many miracles he did before their very eyes.

"If you are the Christ, tell us plainly," they said. Jesus replied, "I have told you, but you do not believe. The works I have done in my Father's name are my witnesses; but you do not believe... "

John 10:24-25

Sometimes I don't welcome the Lord either. He knows about the times I reject him or doubt him. But he is patient. He is always waiting for me to come back to him.

Lord, forgive me for the times when
I turn away from you.
Give me the joy of your forgiveness.
I pray too for those who
refuse to know and love you.
May your Holy Spirit lead them
to peace and truth !

Simon of Cyrene

Jesus was arrested, condemned and beaten. Here he is carrying his cross up to the place where they will crucify him. He was so exhausted that the Roman soldiers pulled a man out of the crowd to help him carry his heavy cross.

> *They seized on a man, Simon from Cyrene,*
> *who was coming in from the country,*
> *and made him shoulder the cross,*
> *and carry it behind Jesus.*
>
> Luke 23:26

Simon didn't choose to help Jesus, he was forced to. He had been working all day. He was tired and he wanted to rest. But he put all his heart and his compassion into it, and this was a great comfort to Jesus. He helped as much with his friendship as with the strength of his arms.

Sometimes when I have to do my homework, tidy up my things, or help around the house - all these things can seem too much for me. Just like Simon, I can choose to put all my heart and all my love into it.

You were not helping a criminal, Simon,
you were helping the Son of God !
When I love someone, I am loving Jesus.
When I help someone, I am helping Jesus.
Teach me to serve others with a smile,
to help those who are sad and to
recognise Jesus in all those who suffer.

The good thief

Jesus was crucified between two criminals. One
of them was furious: if Jesus was the son of God,
he should get them down from there ! The other
criminal answered him harshly, and then said to Jesus:

> *"Jesus... remember me when you come into your*
> *kingdom." "Indeed, I promise you," Jesus replied,*
> *"today you will be with me in paradise."*
>
> Luke 23:42-43

The good thief recognised his faults. He knew
he deserved to be punished for all the bad things
he had done, but he understood that God's love is
stronger than even the worst sins. In spite of all his
wrongdoing, he recognised that Jesus was the Son of
God... So, was the first person to go to heaven really
a criminal ? Yes, but a criminal who had been forgiven !

Lord, I am not a criminal, I am "only" a sinner !
But I too want to open my heart to the love of Jesus
and ask his forgiveness.

Lord, you never stop loving me,
in spite of the times I am selfish, the
times I tell lies, the times I do bad things.
Your mercy is stronger than my sin.
Lord Jesus, thank you
for forgiving me so much.

Mary Magdalene

Mary Magdalene followed Jesus faithfully up to Jerusalem where he was crucified. She stayed there, near his tomb. She was crying. Jesus's body had disappeared, and she really wanted to know where he was. But suddenly the risen Jesus was there ! He was near her, speaking to her ! What a surprise, what an incredible joy !

Go and find the brothers, and tell them I am ascending to my Father and your Father, to my God and your God.

John 20:17

Jesus chose her to announce his resurrection. She was the first witness. She really could announce it to everyone: Jesus is risen. She had seen him !

I haven't seen Jesus ! But I believe the witnesses who did see him and have announced that he is risen. He has triumphed over death and sin !

Glory to you, Lord !
You were dead, and you are risen !
By your passion, your death
and your resurrection, you give us life !
I believe that you live for ever and ever.
Alleluia !

Thomas

After he rose from the dead, Jesus appeared to his disciples, but Thomas wasn't there. He refused to believe them. It was all too incredible for him ! Eight days later Jesus appeared again to the disciples. Thomas was there, and Jesus told him off for his lack of faith.

> *You believe because you can see me. Happy are those who have not seen and yet believe.*
>
> John 20:29

Thomas didn't trust his friends. He needed proof. But worst of all, Thomas didn't trust Jesus. He wanted to see him with his own eyes, and touch him with his hands before he would believe Jesus was risen...

I would like to have proof too ! It would be so much simpler if I could see and touch the Lord. But no: Jesus wants me to believe without seeing.

Lord Jesus, I don't see you with my eyes,
I don't hear you with my ears,
but I believe that you are there
inside me, and in everyone
who believes in you.
Deep down, in the silence,
I want to say to you,
with all my heart:
"My Lord and my God."

43

The disciple Jesus loved

Of course, Jesus loved all his disciples - Peter,
James, Andrew, Bartholomew... But the Gospel
mentions one disciple without telling us his name.
He is just called 'the disciple Jesus loved'. He was
very, very close to Jesus.

> *The disciple Jesus loved was reclining*
> *next to Jesus.*
>
> John 13:23

44

Maybe he was more open to Jesus's word and
to his love ? Maybe he was better at listening, at
welcoming people, at loving them in a special way ?
Perhaps most of all, he was a disciple who was able
to love very deeply.

What kind of disciple am I for Jesus ? He certainly
loves me with a special love; and he wants so much for
me to be able to welcome all his love...

Jesus, your love doesn't make
comparisons or calculations.
You give to everyone
without counting the cost.
Every person is the disciple you love.
Each one is your favourite.
Each one leans on you.
Help me, Jesus, to open my heart.
Make it overflow with your love
so that it can nourish
all the people around me.

Who do you say that I am ?

One day Jesus asked his disciples:

Who do you say that I am ?

What a strange question ! They knew very well
who he was. They lived with him all the time ! But
Jesus wanted to help them to answer truly, from their
hearts and with faith.

Having faith means believing that Jesus is the Son of
God, who came on earth to save us from sin and death.

In the same way that he called his disciples, the
Lord calls me too to follow him, to meet him and love
him. He is the Way, the Truth and the Life. In Jesus
I will find true happiness.

Just as he asked his disciples, so Jesus asks me
today: "Who do you say that I am ?" How shall I
answer ? You are love, life, goodness, peace... Yes, you
are all those things, because you are the Son of the
Living God !

Jesus, God wants to save
me through you !
You are Emmanuel –
through you God is with me.
You are the Word –
through you God speaks to me.
You are the Lamb of God,
full of sweetness and goodness.
You are King of the Universe,
full of mercy and charity.
You are the Light for all men.
To you be Glory and Praise !

CTS Children's Books

The Bible for little children, *by Maïte Roche*
(ISBN 1 86082 399 8 CTS Code CH 2)

The Gospel for little children, *by Maïte Roche*
(ISBN 1 86082 400 5 CTS Code CH 1)

The Rosary, *by Juliette Levivier*
(ISBN 1 86082 397 1 CTS Code CH 3)

The Way of the Cross, *by Juliette Levivier*
(ISBN 1 86082 398 X CTS Code CH 4)

First prayers for little children, *by Maïte Roche*
(ISBN 978 1 86082 443 2 CTS Code CH 5)

Praying with the friends of Jesus, *by Juliette Levivier*
(ISBN 978 1 86082 444 9 CTS Code CH 6)

Prayers around the Crib, *by Juliette Levivier*
(ISBN 978 1 86082 445 6 CTS Code CH 7)

The most beautiful Christmas Story, *by Maïte Roche*
(ISBN 978 1 86082 446 3 CTS Code CH 8)

Faith for children, *by Christine Pedotti*
(ISBN 978 1 86082 447 0 CTS Code CH 9)

Praying with the friends of Jesus: Published 2007 by the Incorporated Catholic Truth Society, 40-46 Harleyford Road, London SE11 5AY. Tel: 020 7640 0042; Fax: 020 7640 0046; www.cts-online.org.uk. Copyright © 2007 The Incorporated Catholic Truth Society in this English-language edition.

ISBN: 978 1 86082 444 9 CTS Code CH 6

Prier avec les amis de Jésus by Juliette Levivier, illustrations by Anne Gravier, published 2006 by Edifa-Mame, 15-27 rue Moussorgski, 75018 Paris; ISBN Edifa 978-2-9145-8094-6; ISBN Mame 978-2-7289-1192-9. Copyright © Groupe Fleurus 2006.